SIMPLE
ORIENTAL
COOKERY

COMPILED BY EDNA BEILENSON
AND WITH DECORATIONS
BY RUTH MCCREA

Peter Pauper Press
MOUNT VERNON · NEW YORK

To the Reader

From China, Hawaii
From the Far- and Near-East,
We bring you these dishes
On which you can feast.

They're really quite simple;
They're really quite good;
And really quite different
From our Western food!

You'll like Sukiyaki
And Chinese Chow Mein;
You'll come back to the curries
Again and again!

So don your kimono
Your sari or lei;
And fix your next party
The old Eastern way!

Chinese Dishes

Egg-Flower Soup

½ cup water chestnuts
1 quart chicken broth
2 eggs
Pepper, salt

Pour half a cupful of finely chopped water chestnuts into a quart of boiling chicken broth and cook for about 5 minutes. Beat the 2 eggs and pour into chicken broth, stirring slowly until small flowers are formed. Add pepper and salt to taste. Serves 4.

Chinese Clear Chicken Soup

(Ting Gai Tong)

4 cups chicken stock
2 tablespoons boiled chicken, diced
Pinch of salt
Pinch of gourmet powder
Dash of pepper

Heat chicken stock, add chicken, salt, gourmet powder and pepper; bring to a boil and serve.

Subgum Chicken Soup

(Subgum Gai Tong)

1 tablespoon canned French mushrooms, chopped
4 cups chicken stock
2 tablespoons Chinese cabbage, chopped
2 tablespoons tomato, chopped
2 tablespoons green pepper, chopped
1 tablespoon peeled water chestnuts, chopped
2 tablespoons boiled chicken, chopped
2 tablespoons canned bamboo shoots, chopped
1 tablespoon celery, chopped
Pinch of salt
Dash of pepper
1 teaspoon gourmet powder
1 beaten egg
2 teaspoons cornstarch

Soak mushrooms about 10 minutes or until soft. Heat stock and add cabbage, tomato, green pepper, water chestnuts, mushrooms, chicken, bamboo shoots, celery, salt, pepper and gourmet powder. Bring to a boil and stir egg into soup; then add cornstarch which has been made into a smooth paste. Stir and cook 2 minutes.

With true friends, even water drunk together, is enough!

6

Watercress Soup

(Saye Yeung Choy Tong)

4 cups chicken stock
2 bunches watercress
½ cup sliced raw lean pork
  (small, thin slices)
½ teaspoon salt
1 teaspoon gourmet powder
1 egg

Heat chicken stock, add watercress, pork, salt and gourmet powder. Bring to a boil, drop in egg to poach and boil 6 minutes.

Bird's Nest Chicken Soup

(Yien Wor Gai Tong)

3 ounces bird's nest
4 cups chicken stock
½ teaspoon salt
1 teaspoon gourmet powder
3 egg whites
3 teaspoons cornstarch
½ teaspoon boiled ham, chopped

Soak bird's nest in water 1 hour, then boil 1 hour in enough water to cover. Wash in cold water and drain. Heat chicken stock, add bird's nest, salt and gourmet powder. Bring to a boil. Add beaten egg whites, stir constantly. Slowly add cornstarch which has been made into a paste. Stir well and cook 2 minutes. Pour into a bowl and sprinkle ham on top.

Sweet and Pungent Sauce

1 tablespoon cornstarch
½ cup brown sugar
⅓ cup vinegar
6 tablespoons pineapple juice
2 teaspoons soy sauce

Put cornstarch and brown sugar in saucepan. Add vinegar, pineapple juice and soy sauce. Bring to boil and simmer 1½ minutes.

Sweet and Pungent Shrimp

1 pound fresh shrimp
½ cup flour
2 eggs
Salt

Remove shells and veins from shrimp and rinse in cold water. Sift flour into beaten eggs, stirring the eggs at the same time, making a smooth paste. Add salt to mixture. Dip shrimp in egg mixture and fry in deep, hot sesame oil.

Prepare Sweet and Pungent Sauce. Add fried shrimp to sauce. Cook for 2 minutes more. Serve immediately.

Sweet and Pungent Halibut
(Dow See Yu)

1½ pounds halibut
2 eggs
Flour

Clean fish. Dip in beaten eggs and dredge in flour. Fry in deep fat, and serve with sweet and pungent sauce poured over.

Fried Shrimp with Ham and Bacon
(Teit Par Ha)

1 pound fresh shrimp
½ cup flour
3 eggs
¼ pound sliced bacon
½ pound boiled ham (sliced medium thick)

Boil shrimp, remove shells and veins and rinse in cold water. Sift flour into beaten eggs and mix into a smooth paste. Cut bacon and ham slices into squares according to size of shrimp. Flatten out the shrimp. On top of each shrimp place a piece of ham then a piece of bacon. Dip in egg mixture. Fry in hot skillet, greased with sesame oil. Brown cakes on both sides.

10

Shrimp Balls

2 pounds shrimp
1 egg white
½ tablespoon cornstarch
1 tablespoon Chinese soy sauce

Boil shrimp. Remove shells and veins and rinse in cold water. Chop coarsely. Mix all ingredients together and shape into balls. Fry in deep hot sesame oil for 6 to 8 minutes. Serve with soy sauce or season with salt and pepper if you prefer. This dish makes a fine hors-d'oeuvre.

Butterfly Shrimp

2 pounds jumbo shrimp
1 pound sliced bacon
Flour
Oil for frying

Clean and shell shrimp and remove black vein. Split each shrimp down the back almost to the tail. Leave on tail. Make 3 slits on inside of shrimp. Slip ½ strip of bacon into slits, weaving in and out. Roll shrimp in flour. Put small amount of oil into frying pan. When hot, fry shrimp for 5 minutes on each side. Serve with Chinese barbecue sauce. *See next page.*

Chinese Barbecue Sauce

¼ cup soy sauce
2 tablespoons honey
1 tablespoon brown sugar
1 teaspoon salt
½ teaspoon pepper
1 piece fresh or dried ginger root,
   1½ inches long, grated
1 garlic clove, minced
½ ounce Brandy

Combine all ingredients and mix well.

Lobster Cantonese

2 large lobsters
2 teaspoons black beans, soaked
4 cloves garlic
8 ounces raw lean pork, chopped
4 tablespoons butter
1 teaspoon salt
Dash of pepper
1 teaspoon sugar
2 teaspoons gourmet powder
2 cups stock or water
4 scallions
4 teaspoons cornstarch
6 eggs, well beaten

Split lobsters in half and cut through shell into 1-inch pieces. Wash black beans

thoroughly; drain and crush with garlic. Add to unshelled lobster pieces and pork and sauté in butter 2 minutes, stirring constantly. Add salt, pepper, sugar, gourmet powder and stock; cover and cook 5 minutes.

Add scallions and cornstarch mixed to a smooth paste with 2 tablespoons cold water. Cook 2 minutes; stir small amount into eggs. Gradually add to cooked mixture, stirring constantly until slightly thickened. Serves 4.

Egg Foo Yung

½ cup cooked ham, minced
½ cup onion, minced
¼ cup water chestnuts, sliced
1 cup bean sprouts
¼ teaspoon salt
5 eggs, well beaten
Fat for frying

Combine ham, onion, water chestnuts and bean sprouts; add salt and eggs, beating until thick. Drop from large spoon into frying pan covered with 1 inch layer of hot fat, and fry about 10 minutes, turning to brown both sides. Drain and serve hot. Serves 6.

Chinese Long White Rice

Soak rice ½ hour. Pour boiling water over the rice until the water is 1½ to 2 inches above the rice. Add salt. Boil 1½ minutes, lower flame and simmer 30 minutes.

Almond Chow Mein

1 pound noodles
¼ pound mushrooms
¼ pound bamboo shoots
¼ pound water chestnuts
⅛ cup chicken meat, thinly sliced
⅛ cup cooked ham, thinly sliced
2 eggs
½ cup roasted almonds

Cook noodles in salted, boiling water for 5 minutes. Drain and run cold water over them. Dry noodles for ½ hour and drop into deep fat. Remove from pot quickly and drain fat off on brown paper. Fry mushrooms, bamboo shoots, and water chestnuts in a greased frying pan until tender, and then season with salt, pepper, soybean sauce and ginger to taste. Remove vegetables from pan, and fry noodles in the same grease.

Next, place a layer of noodles, a layer of vegetables, and a layer of chicken and ham

on a large platter. Beat 2 eggs and fry in a greased pan. Slice very fine, and spread on top of chicken and ham. Sprinkle almonds over the chow mein, and trim with parsley if desired.

Chicken Chop Suey

4 tablespoons peanut oil
2 teaspoons salt
4 cups raw chicken, cut into 1-inch pieces
2 cups water
2 cups celery, cut into 1-inch pieces
24 water chestnuts, sliced
1 pound fresh mushrooms, sliced
2 cups bamboo shoots, sliced
2 cups Chinese greens, cut into 1-inch pieces

Heat peanut oil in a frying pan until very hot. Add salt and the chicken. Cook until brown, then add water and all other ingredients. Cover and cook for 20 minutes. Add sauce.

Sauce:

2 tablespoons soy sauce
3 teaspoons cornstarch
1 teaspoon sugar
1 jigger Whisky or Brandy
1 cup water

Stir all together until thickened. Serve with rice or fried noodles. Serves 6.

Diced Chicken with Walnuts

1 cup English walnut halves
Vegetable shortening
1 young chicken (3½ lbs.)
1 cup clear chicken broth
1 cup green peas
1 cup celery, diced
1 cup carrots, diced
½ cup mushrooms, diced
½ pound Chinese white vegetable
  (Bok Choy), diced
¼ cup water chestnuts, diced
¼ cup canned bamboo shoots, diced
1½ teaspoons salt
Dash of pepper
1 teaspoon sugar
1 teaspoon gourmet powder
2 teaspoons Sherry
3 teaspoons cornstarch

Deep fry walnuts in ½ cup vegetable shortening until delicately brown. Drain and put aside.

Disjoint chicken and remove all bones. Dice chicken, then sauté in vegetable shortening or butter for 2 minutes. Add ¼ cup chicken broth, all the vegetables, salt, pepper, sugar, and gourmet powder. Cook for 10 minutes. Add ¾ cup chicken broth and the Sherry, and pour mixture into pot. Stir well. Thicken with cornstarch paste. Simmer for 2 minutes. Stir in the walnuts. Serves 6.

Chinese Chicken and Rice

1 chicken (4-5 lbs.)
Soy sauce
2 small onions
2 cups uncooked rice
½ cup peanuts
½ cup almonds
1 cup bread cubes
1 cup raisins
1 pint chicken stock
Cornstarch for thickening
¼ cup pine seeds
¼ cup shredded coconut

Boil the chicken whole. Add soy sauce and the onions. Steam or boil rice. Remove skin from chicken, break meat into small pieces, then set dish in hot water to keep warm. Fry nuts and bread cubes in deep fat. Pile rice after mixing in raisins on a large platter. Surround with nuts and bread cubes. Put chicken on top and pour over it 1 pint of chicken stock thickened with cornstarch. Sprinkle pine seed and coconut over top.

Duck and Pineapple Cantonese

1 duck (5-6 lbs.)
1/4 cup shoyu sauce
1 tablespoon sugar
1/2 teaspoon salt
1 ground ginger root
1 clove garlic
1/4 cup cooking oil
2 cups water
1 cup syrup from canned pineapple
2 tablespoons cornstarch
1/4 cup water
2 cups pineapple, diced

Wash duck and cut in pieces for stewing; dip in mixture of shoyu sauce, sugar, salt and ginger root and add with garlic to oil in heavy frying pan. Sauté 15 minutes, or until well browned; add water and pineapple juice and simmer, covered, 1 hour, or until tender.

Remove duck to hot platter and keep hot. Mix cornstarch and water to a paste, stir into hot liquid in pan and cook 10 minutes, stirring until thickened; add pineapple, cook 5 minutes longer. Turn sauce over stewed duck and serve piping hot. Serves 6.

Food cures hunger; study cures ignorance!

Pekin Duck

1 duck (5-6 lbs.)
4 teaspoons honey
½ cup hot water
2 teaspoons rose wine
1 teaspoon fried salt

Wash and clean duck. Scald by dipping in hot water, and hang up to dry. Mix honey with hot water, rub well into the duck's skin, and allow to dry until skin is hard. This will take about 10 hours.

Mix wine and fried salt. Pour into the inside of the duck. Roast in oven about 1 hour. Slice the skin from the roast duck in 2-inch squares and serve separately. Then slice meat from breast, legs and wings. Serves 4.

Roast Duck with Orange Sauce

1 duck (5-6 lbs.)
Anise oil → cooked
3 cups white rice
½ pound bulk sausage
1 stalk celery, finely chopped
1 onion, chopped
1 small can crushed pineapple
Seasoning to taste
Sliced almonds

*Score the ¼ inch ↑ squares
skin in   and salt (outside only)*

Wash duck and wipe dry. Rub inside and
outside with anise oil, then let stand for
1 hour while preparing dressing. (Cook
giblets separately and save stock.) Cook
and steam the rice until tender. Fry sausage meat with celery and onion until
golden brown. Add hot rice to sausage
mixture. Add pineapple. Finally add 3 or
4 drops of anise oil, or 1 teaspoon anise
seed instead.

Fill duck with the above dressing. Roast
in open roasting pan for about 2½ hours,
or until tender, at 350°. Before serving,
garnish with sliced almonds, and serve
with orange sauce.

Orange Sauce:
2 cups orange juice
1 cup broth from giblets
½ teaspoon orange rind, grated
2 tablespoons white vinegar
½ cup sugar
Cornstarch

Cook all ingredients in double boiler and
thicken with cornstarch until the consist-
ency of heavy cream. Serve separately,
and ladle over duck. Serves 6.

*All the world over, people enjoy salt and
money!*

23

Sweet and Sour Pork

1 cup flour
4 eggs, slightly beaten
1 teaspoon salt
2 pounds lean pork, cut into 1-inch cubes
Oil for frying
2 cups pineapple chunks
12 small sweet pickles, sliced
2 green peppers, cut into 1-inch squares
6 carrots, sliced
2 cloves garlic, chopped fine
2 cups water
4 tablespoons vinegar
3 tablespoons sugar
2 tablespoons molasses
2 tablespoons cornstarch

Mix flour, eggs and salt to make a batter. Dip the cubed pork into batter. Fry in deep hot oil for 10 minutes. Remove and drain on absorbent paper. Put pork cubes into frying pan, add pineapple, sweet pickles, green peppers, carrots, garlic and 1 cup water. Cook covered for 12 minutes. Combine the vinegar, sugar, molasses, cornstarch and 1 cup of water and blend thoroughly. Mix well with the meat and cook for another 8 minutes. Serves 8.

If you want dinner, don't insult the cook!

Sweet-and-Sour Meat Balls

(Tim Shun Yok Kow)

4 medium green peppers, seeded
4 canned pineapple slices
1 pound ground chuck
2 teaspoons soy sauce
Salt
1 teaspoon seasoned salt
¼ teaspoon pepper
1 tablespoon flour
2 tablespoons butter
1 cup chicken broth
½ cup juice from pineapple
¼ cup vinegar
2 tablespoons cornstarch
1 tablespoon sugar
2 teaspoons soy sauce
Hot rice or canned chow mein noodles

Cut each pepper into six pieces; cook, in boiling water to cover, 3 minutes; drain. Cut each pineapple slice into 6 pieces; drain. Combine chuck, 2 teaspoons soy sauce, ¾ teaspoon salt, seasoned salt, pepper; blend well. Shape into 16 small balls; roll balls in flour. In hot butter in skillet over medium heat, brown balls on all sides; cover; simmer 5 minutes, remove to hot platter; keep warm.

To butter in skillet, add ⅓ cup chicken

broth, green peppers, pineapple pieces. Cover; simmer 8 minutes. Meanwhile, combine ⅔ cup broth, pineapple juice, vinegar, cornstarch, sugar, 2 teaspoons soy sauce, ½ teaspoon salt; add to green-pepper mixture; stir constantly till thickened and clear. Pour pepper mixture over meat balls. Serve hot, with rice or chow mein noodles. Serves 4.

Pepper Steak with Tomatoes

1 pound flank steak
1 pound green peppers
1 pound tomatoes
½ pound onions
2 cloves garlic
3 teaspoons cornstarch
1 cup chicken broth
3 tablespoons fat
1 teaspoon salt
1 teaspoon sugar
1 teaspoon gourmet powder
2 teaspoons soy sauce
2 teaspoons spiced black soybeans (optional)

Trim steak and wipe clean. Slice cross-grained to obtain thin slices 3 inches by 1 inch by ⅛ inch. Cut peppers, tomatoes and onions into eighths. Crush garlic. Mix cornstarch with ½ cup of broth.

Sauté garlic in 3 tablespoons hot fat until slightly brown. Stir in flank steak turning on high flame for 2 minutes. Put steak into a warm bowl and put aside while sauce is cooking.

Sauté onions and peppers for 5 minutes, then add tomatoes, salt, sugar, gourmet powder, soy sauce, ½ cup of broth. Cover and cook vigorously for 2 minutes. Add cornstarch mixture. Stir, cover, and simmer 2 minutes. Add steak gradually. Serves 6.

Shoyu Steak

2 pounds round steak
1 cup shoyu
1 piece ginger root, mashed
½ cup flour
4 tablespoons fat
1 large onion, sliced

Cut meat into pieces for serving. Soak in shoyu and mashed ginger for 1 hour or more. Drain. Roll in flour. Brown in fat. Add onion, sliced and browned. Remove meat and make gravy using shoyu as part of liquid. Serves 6.

You can't fill your belly painting pictures of bread!

Almond Cakes

2 teaspoons almond extract
4 cups shortening
8 cups all-purpose flour, sifted
3 cups sugar
3 teaspoons salt
Blanched almond halves

Blend almond extract into shortening, creaming until soft. Gradually work in flour, then sugar and salt. Knead to a paste. Form into a thick roll, then cut in ½-inch slices.

Arrange on ungreased cookie sheet, press an almond half into center of each and bake in a 300° oven about 30 minutes. Yields 40 cakes.

Japanese Dishes

Japanese Rice
(Gohan)

2 cups rice
2½ cups water
1 teaspoon salt

Wash rice in a sieve under running water,

shaking until the water runs clear. Place rice, water, and salt in a heavy kettle with a tight-fitting lid. Cook without stirring over a low flame for 25 minutes. Remove from the fire. Serves 6.

Sukiyaki

3 cups canned bamboo sprouts
3 cups canned or cooked dried mushrooms
3 white onions
1 bunch green onions
½ bunch leeks
3 stalks celery
3 pounds spinach or string beans
3 squares bean curd
1½ pounds round steak
⅓ cup shoyu sauce
½ teaspoon Accent
3 tablespoons sugar
⅓ cup mushroom liquor
¾ cup salad oil
10-12 cups hot, cooked rice

Slice bamboo sprouts, mushrooms and white onions very fine; cut green onions, leeks and celery diagonally into 2-inch strips, using green tops of onions and leeks; shred the spinach or string beans and cut bean curd in 1-inch cubes. Arrange separately in neat piles on large platters ready for cooking on grill. Cut meat crossgrain in paper-thin slices and spread out on platter.

For sauce, simmer shoyu, Accent, sugar and mushroom liquor for 3 minutes.

Brown onions slightly in piping hot oil in heavy frying pan over grill, at table; add vegetables and bean curd, and cook 1 minute; then add 1/2 of sauce. When hot, add meat, spreading it out thin; cook over low flame 15 minutes, stirring occasionally and adding remaining sauce as it is needed.

Reduce heat and serve directly from pan on hot boiled rice in individual bowls. Serves 12.

Chicken Satsuma

2 broiling chickens, cut in small pieces
3 carrots, diced
3 parsnips, diced
3 potatoes, diced
Shoyu

Place chickens and vegetables in an iron pot. Barely cover with water. Season with shoyu. Cover and simmer until tender, removing scum from time to time. Serve with rice. Serves 6.

Mizutaki

1 chicken (3 lbs.)
Chicken stock or water to cover
Salt
6 scallions, cut in 1-inch lengths
1 medium-size onion, peeled and sliced thin
1 bunch watercress, trimmed
1 cup lemon juice
1 cup soy sauce
1 cup Japanese wine (sake)
1 level teaspoon Accent

Have the butcher divide the chicken in half and cut or chop it into 1½-inch cubes with bones. Place the pieces in a heavy saucepan and cover with chicken stock or water. Add a little salt and simmer gently for 1 hour. Bring to the table in cooking utensil and place over a charcoal or alcohol burner so that the liquid barely boils.

When guests are seated, commence adding vegetables to the simmering broth, a few at a time. To serve, spoon a few portions of the meat and barely cooked vegetables into small serving bowls. Using chopsticks or forks, guests dip bite-sized bits of chicken into a sauce made by combining lemon juice, soy sauce, sake and Accent. Serve with hot cooked rice. Serves 4.

Shrimp or Fish Fritters

(*Tempura*)

1 cup flour
1/2 teaspoon salt
2/3 cup milk
2 eggs, beaten
2 cups large shrimp or other fish
Deep fat

Sift flour with salt. Add milk and eggs. Dip shrimp or other fish in batter. Fry in deep fat at 375° until golden brown.

Note: Crabs, lobsters, scallops, and smelts are commonly used for fish *tempura.* Vegetables, fried separately, may be cooked by the above method.

Japanese Sweet Fritters

2 eggs
1 cup sugar
1 cup milk
3 cups flour
1 teaspoon baking powder
Salt
Nutmeg
Lard for frying

Combine ingredients, and flavor strongly with nutmeg. Fry in hot lard. Yield: 2 1/2 to 3 dozen.

Hawaiian and Indonesian Dishes

Chicken Luau

1 fowl (4-5 lbs.)
Salt
Butter
2 cups milk
2 cups fresh coconut, grated
Flour
3 pounds spinach, cooked

Cut fowl as for stewing. Cook until tender. Season with salt and butter. Mix the milk and coconut and boil in a double boiler. Strain. Make a gravy with the coconut milk, slightly thickening with flour. Pour over fowl. Serve with spinach. Serves 6.

Hawaiian Curry

1 coconut, grated
4 cups milk
1 tablespoon onion, chopped
2 tablespoons butter
1 tablespoon curry powder (scant)
1 teaspoon ginger, ground
Fish, chicken, or lamb

Grate coconut and soak in milk for 1 hour.

Fry onion in butter until brown, then add to the onion the curry and the ginger. Strain off the milk from the coconut, and pour it over the mixture in the frying pan. Put in the raw chicken, fish, or meat and cook slowly until done.

Serve with salted peanuts, grated coconut, chutney, preserves or finely chopped bacon, fried crisp.

Hawaiian Pork Chops

4 loin pork chops
Salt and pepper
Flour
4 slices pineapple, canned
4 pitted prunes
4 carrots
1/3 cup water

Wipe chops and season with salt and pepper. Dust with flour, and place in pan. Upon each chop place a ring of pineapple with a pitted prune in the center. Between chops, place whole carrots, and add water. Cover. Cook slowly for 1½ hours. Remove to hot platter. Make a gravy from mixture in pan. Pour over chops. Garnish with parsley. Serves 4.

Hawaiian Papaya Freeze

1 cup sugar
½ tablespoon lemon juice
1½ cups orange juice
1 cup papaya pulp
2 cups rich milk

Mix sugar, fruit juices and papaya pulp and chill thoroughly; gradually stir into milk and freeze in an ice cream freezer. If papaya is out of season, use 1 cup papaya marmalade and omit sugar. Serves 8.

Javanese Bamie

4 pork chops
4 onions
1 bunch scallions
Garlic, crushed
1 bunch parsley
1 white cabbage (small)
1 bunch celery
1 can beansprouts
½ pound shrimp or 1 can shrimp — *use*
Soy sauce
½ pound noodles — *cook first*
1 lemon, quartered
4 eggs

Cut all ingredients, meat included, into small pieces. Fry the pork squares until dark brown, fry the onions separately, put them together in heavy skillet, add crushed garlic, then the other vegetables and the shrimp, and add 2 tablespoons of soy sauce. Do not cook too long.

Cook the noodles and add these last. Serve with pieces of lemon and top each individual plate with fried egg. Serves 4.

Note: It is important not to overcook this dish, and the vegetables should retain part of their original crispness.

Nasi Goreng

2 cups of long-grained rice
3 onions, diced
Garlic, crushed
1 green pepper, diced
Vegetable shortening
2 cups leftover pork, ham or any other
  meat, cut small
2 pounds shrimp, fried
2 cucumbers
6 eggs

Wash rice well, cover with cold water standing 1 inch above rice. Cook quickly on rather high flame until there is no water left (tilt pot to see if there is any water left on the bottom) and little dents have appeared on the surface. Cover tight, put on lowest flame, using asbestos cover on burner and cook at this low heat for at least 1 hour. It is very important that rice be dry, not soggy.

Mix cut onions, crushed garlic and cut green pepper in heavy skillet and fry in shortening until golden brown. Add meat, then the rice by tablespoonfuls and fry over small flame, until mixture is light brown in color. Do not stir, but lift with spatula, so as not to crush the rice kernels.

To serve: Place on large platter, arrange large fried shrimp and pieces of cucumber (either slices or strips) on the side. Put a fried egg on top of each individual serving and eat it with spoon and fork. Serves 6.

Eggplant, Javanese

1 eggplant
½ cup milk
½ cup flour
Butter for frying
3 tomatoes
5 ounces sweet butter
2 shallots, chopped
1 cup cream sauce
2 egg yolks
1 pinch parsley, chopped
Salt and pepper
Parmesan cheese as needed

Cut 1 medium size eggplant into slices about 1 inch thick; dip in milk, dredge with flour and fry in butter, seasoned with salt.

Prepare Sauce Portugaise: Peel about 3 tomatoes, remove seeds and chop. Melt 2 ounces of sweet butter and add 2 shallots chopped fine; sauté until golden brown, add the tomatoes and chopped parsley. Cook for 10 minutes and thicken with 1 cup of cream sauce, 2 egg yolks and 3 ounces of sweet butter added a little at a time, and seasoned with salt and pepper.

When the sauce is ready pour a little into a casserole and arrange slices of eggplant in it. Pour a little sauce over them. Then place a second layer of eggplant and over them pour the remaining sauce. Sprinkle grated Parmesan cheese over all and place under broiler to brown. Serves 4.

Too much talk, beware trouble! Too much food, beware indigestion!

Indian Dishes

Pilau

1 cup butter
2 medium onions, sliced
1 cup rice
2 tablespoons seedless raisins
1 tablespoon almonds
Few small pieces cinnamon
Few cardamoms
1 or 2 bay leaves
Salt
Peppercorns
Saffron

Put 4 tablespoons of butter in a saucepan and, when hot, fry the sliced onions to a golden brown. Then add the rice, with the rest of the butter, and cook till the rice has absorbed most of the butter, stirring frequently. Then add the other ingredients and just cover with hot water. Cook and simmer very gently till the rice is tender.

Remove the rice from the saucepan, put in the oven so that the moisture will evaporate. Ten minutes before serving sprinkle with saffron. Serves 6.

Chicken Pulao

1 cup butter
4 large onions, sliced
1 medium-sized chicken,
   cut into serving pieces
1 pound soup beef
Ginger
Salt
2 cloves garlic
2 tablespoons blanched almonds
3 tablespoons seedless raisins
2 sticks cinnamon
Few cardamoms
1 blade mace
6 cloves
Peppercorns
1 cup rice
Saffron

Melt the butter, add 2 sliced onions and fry to a light brown. Next add the chicken, previously boiled in water, with a piece of beef, 2 sliced onions, a little ginger, and salt. Cook till evenly browned, adding the other ingredients and spices, except the rice and saffron.

Then add the rice and sufficient chicken stock (the water in which the chicken was cooked) to cover. Put the lid on the pan and simmer very slowly. Add the saffron when the rice is nearly cooked. To serve, put the chicken on a hot dish, and cover with the rice. A garnish of sliced hard-boiled eggs is sometimes added.

Indian Kabab Curry

¾ pound beef, mutton, or veal
4 onions
2 tablespoons green ginger
2 cloves garlic, chopped
4 tablespoons butter
1 tablespoon curry powder
Salt
Hot water
½ pound tomatoes

Cut the meat into inch lengths and onions in pieces of about the same size. Slice the ginger. Put the pieces of meat on skewers, alternating with pieces of onion and ginger. Brown the remaining onions and the chopped garlic in butter and when brown stir in the curry powder and salt. Add 3 tablespoons of hot water and simmer till reduced. Then add 4 tablespoons of hot water, and the tomatoes divided into quarters. Mix all well and add the meat on the skewers. Simmer for about ¾ hour.

Looking for fish? Don't climb a tree!

Madras Curry

3 small onions
Butter
2 cloves garlic, chopped
1 tablespoon curry powder
Salt
2 cups stock
1 pound mutton, beef, or veal,
    cut into 1-inch cubes
Juice of 1/2 lemon

Slice the onions and fry till golden brown in butter with the chopped garlic. Add the curry powder, and season with salt. Mix well, add the stock and simmer for about 20 minutes. Then add the meat, and simmer for 1 hour or until the meat is quite tender. Just before serving add the juice of 1/2 a lemon.

Cooked meat may be used. In such a case, add to the sauce 15 or 20 minutes before serving.

Indian Rice

(Chowl)

Wash the rice thoroughly in cold water to free it from all loose starch. Put 1 cupful of rice in a large saucepan of boiling salted water, bring again to a full boil, and boil exactly 13 minutes. Then put the rice in a sieve, pour cold water over it, and toss lightly with a fork before serving. Be sure it is piping hot!

Indian Shrimp Curry

3 onions, sliced
2 cloves garlic
4 tablespoons butter
½ tablespoon curry powder
Salt
½ pound tomatoes
Hot water
1 pint cooked shrimp, shelled

Fry the sliced onions and garlic in butter and when brown mix in the curry powder and salt. Quarter the tomatoes and add them, crushing them with a spoon, so as to extract the juice. Add 2 tablespoons of hot water, the shelled shrimp and simmer for 20 minutes.

Other vegetables may be substituted for tomatoes. Shrimp and lentils, or shrimp and eggplant, are frequently combined.

In every family's cooking pot, one black spot!

Chicken Curry
(Northern India)

2 small onions, finely chopped
2 cloves garlic, finely chopped
8 tablespoons butter
1½ teaspoons salt
1 teaspoon turmeric
1 teaspoon chillies
½ teaspoon ground ginger
1 chicken, cut into 8 or 10 pieces
2 cups hot water

Fry the onions and garlic in the butter till well browned, and add the condiments, stirring in with the onions and garlic. When well mixed, add the chicken, divided into joints, and cook till light brown in color. Add the hot water and simmer till the chicken is quite tender and the sauce is reduced to half its original quantity. Serve with rice. Serves 6.

Chicken Dopiaza

3 small onions, sliced
6 tablespoons butter
1 tablespoon curry powder
1 medium-sized chicken, cut into 16 pieces
1 cup hot water

Fry the sliced onions in the hot butter to a golden brown, remove from the pan,

and set aside. Add the curry powder and stir thoroughly Then add the pieces of chicken and fry to a rich brown. Chop the fried onion, add to the chicken, and add the cup of hot water. Simmer for 1 hour or more, until chicken is tender and the sauce is greatly reduced. Serve with rice. Serves 6.

Bombay Salad

1 bunch watercress
4 firm ripe tomatoes
1 cup celery, diced
1 egg yolk, hard-boiled
1 tablespoon chutney
Salt and pepper
3 tablespoons oil
1 tablespoon lemon juice
Lettuce

Pick over watercress, peel tomatoes and cut in pieces, add diced celery, and chill.

Dressing:

Press egg yolk through a sieve, add chutney, salt and pepper, and carefully work in oil with lemon juice. Beat until smooth. Arrange salad on lettuce and pour the dressing over it.

Indian Salad

2 packages lemon jello
1/2 coconut, grated
2 apples, cored and chopped
2 cups celery, chopped
3 pimientos
1 tablespoon onion, grated
1/3 teaspoon salt

Cook jello, following directions on package, and allow a small amount to harden in molds. Fill molds with a mixture of coconut, apples, celery, pimientos, onion, and salt. Pour liquid lemon jello over the fruit. When jelled, turn out the contents of the molds on salad dishes, and sprinkle with grated coconut. Garnish with lettuce, mayonnaise, and pimientos.

Indian Fritters

(Goolgoola)

3 tablespoons flour
Boiling water
4 egg yolks, beaten
4 egg whites, beaten stiff
Hot vegetable shortening
Preserves or marmalade

Put flour in a bowl. Pour enough boiling water over the flour to make a thick paste.

Stir well and do not let the mixture get lumpy. Cool. Add beaten yolks, fold in whites, and mix well. Drop from a tablespoon into boiling hot shortening. Fry until brown. Serve with a spoonful of preserves or marmalade dropped into each fritter. Yield: 2 dozen.

Apple Chutney

4 pounds cooking apples, peeled and cored
4 pounds sugar
1 pound seedless raisins
½ pound mustard seed
½ pound salt
½ pound blanched almonds
⅓ pound chillies
1 pound green ginger
½ clove garlic
3 pints vinegar

Slice the peeled and cored apples into long and thin pieces, put them in a saucepan with 2 pounds of sugar and a little water, and cook till very soft. When cold, place in a bowl and mix in the other ingredients except vinegar. Make a thick syrup with the remaining sugar and the vinegar, and pour over the apples. Cool, and pack in sterile jars.

Divide an orange! It tastes just as good!

Near-Eastern Dishes

Arabian Meat and Eggplant
(Muk-Lou-Beh)

1 pound beef or mutton
Butter
2 large eggplants   *1 sm*
10 cups water   *1 1/3 —*
Saffron, allspice, salt, pepper — *Sprinkle on*
4 cups brown rice   *1/2 C →*
Pine nuts

Chop meat finely and sauté in hot butter.
Spread a thin layer over the bottom of a
large saucepan. Slice eggplant and sauté
to a light brown. Put layer of eggplant
over meat, and alternate layers until ingredients are used up. In 10 cups of water
boil all of the condiments a few minutes.

Wash the raw rice and spread evenly over
the layers of eggplant and meat. Strain
spiced water over the rice. Cook slowly
until rice is done. Melt some butter and
pour over the rice. Turn out onto a large
hot platter, molded into the form of the
saucepan. Garnish with fried pine nuts.

*One day without food and a husband grows
cold!*

Put in casserole, covered @ 300°; bake 1 hr.

54

Levantine Roast Squab With Eggplant

(Patlidjanliguverjin Kezartma)

8 squabs
¾ cup rice, cooked
4 medium onions, chopped
1 bunch parsley, chopped
3 tablespoons butter
Salt, pepper
8 large, round eggplants

Clean squabs and stuff with a mixture of cooked rice, chopped onion and parsley, butter, salt and pepper. Rub each bird with butter and season to taste.

Hollow out the eggplants and place the squabs inside. Arrange in a deep flat pan and bake in a 350° oven until the eggplants are well done. Serve hot with the natural gravy. Serves 8.

Armenian Shish-Kebab

½ pound filet of beef, mutton or lamb
1 medium onion
Pinch of thyme
2 cups broth

Cut meat in walnut-sized pieces. Chop onion very fine, mix with thyme, spread over meat, salt and pepper to taste. Allow meat to stand 3 hours.

Arrange meat on iron skewers and broil over a strong fire. Have ready a hot broth in which to place the broiled Kebabs. When broiling is finished place the vessel containing the broth and Kebabs over a slow fire and allow to simmer for 15 to 20 minutes. Serve hot.

Levantine Boiled Fish
(*Baluck Hashlama*)

4 pounds fish fillets
2 heads garlic, crushed
4 tablespoons olive oil
1 cup water
1 cup white wine
Juice of 4 lemons
1 large bunch parsley
Salt, pepper

Salt fish fillets and allow to stand for 2 hours. When ready, wash and dry each fillet. Crush garlic and fry in a deep skillet with the olive oil. Over this lay the fish. Add water, white wine, lemon juice and parsley. Season to taste and boil over a moderate flame.

Syrian Roast Leg of Lamb

(Kouzou Karni Doldurma)

Leg of lamb (6-7 lbs.)
2 cups prunes, pitted and chopped
1 cup dried figs, chopped
4 tablespoons citron, chopped
¾ cup seeded raisins
½ pound salt pork, finely ground
Thyme, sage, pepper, salt
Coarse, dry bread crumbs
Butter
1 cup hot water
2-3 bay leaves
3 whole peppers
1 tablespoon Worcestershire sauce

Remove bone from leg of lamb making as large a pocket as possible. Mix all ingredients, except last five, together and fill the pocket with the mixture. Sew ends together leaving a small opening for juices to penetrate. Rub meat well with butter and place in a large baking pan. Add hot water, bay leaves, peppers and Worcestershire sauce. Roast at 325° for 3 hours basting frequently.

Serve with rice and eggplant. Serves 8 generously.

Silly toad: planning a meal of goose!

Stuffed Grape Leaves

1 quart jar grape leaves
2 pounds lean lamb, ground
1 cup rice, washed and drained
Pepper to taste
2 teaspoons thyme
1 teaspoon oregano
1 small onion, grated
3 large onions, sliced
2 tablespoons butter
2 No. 3 cans tomatoes

Wash the grape leaves thoroughly in cold water to remove salt. Mix the meat, rice, pepper, thyme, oregano and grated onion. In a large kettle sauté the sliced onions in butter until yellow. Add 1 can of tomatoes and heat. Stuff the grape leaves loosely with the meat mixture, using about 1 tablespoon of the mixture for each leaf. Shake each into a neat package. Place gently in the hot tomato sauce.

Heat the second can of tomatoes and pour over all. Cover and simmer for 1 hour. Serves 6.

Caution: No salt should be added to this dish as the grape leaves are salty.

Mistress slack; servant sloven!

Cucumbers with Yoghurt

(Maste Khiar)

4 cucumbers
¼ cup fresh mint, chopped
3 eight-ounce containers plain yoghurt
Salt, freshly ground pepper

Peel cucumbers and cut into small cubes. Add mint, 2 containers of the yoghurt and salt and pepper to taste. Mix and chill exactly 2 hours. Drain off excess water and add the remaining container of yoghurt. Stir the mixture and chill briefly. Yields 1 quart of salad. Serve with fresh mint.

Lamb and Parsley Stew

(Gormeh Sabzee)

4 large bunches parsley, chopped
16 scallions, chopped
6 tablespoons butter
3 pounds lean lamb, cubed
Salt and pepper
3 lemons
2 No. 2 cans red kidney beans

In a heavy 4-quart pot, sauté the parsley and scallions in 4 tablespoons of the butter until the parsley is dark green. In a large skillet sauté the lamb in the remaining butter until it is lightly browned. Salt and pepper the lamb. Combine lamb with the vegetable mixture in the pot. Add water to cover, the juice of 2 lemons and quarters of the third. Cover and simmer until almost tender, 1 to 1½ hours. Add the kidney beans. Taste and correct seasonings. Continue cooking until the lamb is tender. Serve with Pilau. Serves 6.

Lamb and Vegetable Stew

(Tasskebab)

3 tablespoons butter
2 pounds carrots, cut into ½-inch chunks
6 potatoes, peeled and cut in ½-inch slices
3 pounds lean lamb, cut into 1½-inch cubes
1 teaspoon thyme
1 teaspoon oregano
Salt
Freshly ground black pepper
6 large onions, sliced ½-inch thick
1 No. 3 can Italian tomatoes

In a large pot melt the butter. Turn off heat and arrange in layers the carrots, potatoes and lamb. Add thyme, oregano, salt and pepper to taste, onions and tomatoes. Cover and simmer slowly until the lamb is tender, about 1½ hours. Serve over rice. Serves 6.

THIS VOLUME
HAS BEEN PREPARED
PRINTED AND PUBLISHED
AT THE OFFICE OF
THE PETER PAUPER PRESS
MOUNT VERNON
NEW YORK